Twenty Yesses

Reflections on the Rosary and Its Mysteries

by Rev, Dennis M. McNeil

Nihil obstat:	Reverend Mark A. Latkovich, PhD
	Censor deputatus
Imprimatur:	Most Reverend Edward C. Malesic, JCL
	Bishop of Cleveland

Given at Cleveland, Ohio, on September 10, 2021

The *Nihil obstat* and *Imprimatur* are official declarations that a book or pamphlet is free of doctrinal or moral error. No implication is contained therein that those who have granted the *Nihil obstat* and *imprimatur* agree with the contents, opinions, or statements expressed.

DORRANCE
PUBLISHING CO
EST. 1920
PITTSBURGH, PENNSYLVANIA 15238

Dorrance Publishing Co
585 Alpha Drive
Pittsburgh, PA 15238
Visit our website at *www.dorrancebookstore.com*

ISBN: 978-1-6853-7117-3
ESIBN: 978-1-6853-7962-9

Dedication

To Brother Daniel Adams
and
To Brother Joseph Mussa

Fellow "inmates" who encouraged me to write.

Tom,

Blessings to you always!
I've always been thankful
for your joy!
May Mary's example
   always be a source of
Grace!

   In Christ,
      Dennis Nebr
         Styx

Twenty Yesses

Reflections on the Rosary and Its Mysteries

It doesn't seem necessary to explain why I came back to praying the Rosary regularly except to say that I did. The Rosary has become very dear to me, perhaps as it never had been even when I still prayed it daily.

Brother Michael R., a Marianist brother at Cathedral Latin School in Cleveland, Ohio, taught both religion and math, and I had him almost every year of high school for at least one and sometimes two classes. I vividly remember on November 22, 1963 when the announcement came over the PA system that President Kennedy had been shot. He said that if the president died it would continue the coincidence that every president elected in a year divisible by 20 died in office. Thankfully, though President Reagan (elected in 1980) was shot, he did not die, and the connection was severed.

In any case, Brother Michael, obviously devoted to the Rosary, challenged all of us in his classes to carry the beads every day and that if he found we didn't have them we'd have to say a Rosary for him, and if we found he didn't have them he'd be obliged to pray one for us. If I recall correctly, I caught him three times and he only caught me once! I've been very conscientious since then in carrying a rosary although praying it, not so much.

I was invested in the Brown Scapular of Our Lady of Mount Carmel at my First Communion but hadn't worn it in many years until I read a book on the Blue Army when I was in my deacon year at the seminary. Though I have worn the scapular daily since then, I still didn't get back to praying the Rosary.

But now that I've begun to pray it conscientiously each day and have found it most consoling and important. My reflections have led me to the conclusion that the Mysteries of the Rosary, including the Luminous Mysteries proposed for our use by Pope Saint John Paul II, are ALL about Yes, thus the title of this work.

Sometimes the yes is the yes of Jesus himself, sometimes of Mary and sometimes of other individuals either directly or indirectly involved in the events, but all lead to other yesses. There are more than twenty, of course, but counting them would be a fool's errand, and twenty is a good start. It's my hope that you will find these reflections helpful for your own prayer and for appreciating the great gift that the Rosary is to us, children of the Father and brothers and sisters of Jesus because of Mary's yes, the first Joyful Mystery.

Joyful Mysteries
THE ANNUNCIATION

IT ISN'T DIFFICULT, I THINK, TO SEE YES! IN THIS FIRST mystery. One might well think of Mary's response to Gabriel—and thus to God Himself—and her yes *is* essential. In a society where instant gratification is the norm rather than the exception, we have hundreds of choices. On the two and a half mile stretch of a main road near one parish assignment, there were many restaurants including fast food places like McDonalds, Wendy's, and Burger King as well as several pizza places, family/chain restaurants including Steak 'n' Shake, Applebees, Bob Evans, and Panera, and several independent restaurants like Mucho Bueno (Mexican) and two different Chinese places. You could flip a coin to decide where to eat without a second thought.

God however is different. He chose one specific woman in one particular moment in history to bear His Son. He blessed her with sinlessness from the first moment of her life in her mother's womb but never took her freedom from her! When the angel came, she could certainly have said no, and salvation would have had to be accomplished some other way; the Incarnation would not have happened because He wouldn't just have chosen someone else. He chose Mary and His is the first *Yes!*

He wanted to make it possible for every Son of Adam or Daughter of Eve to come into a saving relationship with Him. He didn't decide Adam and Eve were a lost cause and erased them from existence and flip a coin to start everything all over again with some other kind of creature. It was His decision—the decision of all Three Persons in perfect harmony—to send His Son to become one of us and to show us how to live as daughters and sons. Even knowing that Jesus would be rejected and crucified, He still said *Yes!* for us.

So it is that He sent Gabriel (whose name means "God's Strength") to the woman He chose. While the angel (as angels usually do) said, "Fear not!" I don't think that fear entered Mary's mind or heart at all. Startled I'm sure she was, for angels don't generally appear every day, but her relationship of trust in the God she loved was total. Fear, I believe, often comes through awareness that we are sinners and far less than we ought to be, but Mary was not conscious of that.

She knew this messenger was from God and after asking the reasonable question, "How can this be?" was satisfied with Gabriel's answer, and she responded with the most important *Yes!* for our salvation. Her *fiat—let it be done to me according to your will—*made it possible for the Word to become Flesh and to dwell among us. Her *Yes!* made Jesus one of us, sharing the fullness of our humanity, including our mortality.

That yes was profound; she couldn't possibly have understood all of its implications or the suffering it would bring her, and yet she gave it freely and willingly. It was the first of many that would be asked of her and that she would continue to give.

May the Father, Son and Holy Spirit help us to surrender our wills to the Will of the Trinity, as Mary did, so that we can make Christ present in all of our circumstances.

The Visitation

SOME YEARS AGO, WHILE SEARCHING FOR A PICTURE OF THE visitation, I came upon (and fell in love with) "Jump for Joy" by Corby Eisbacher (when I wrote this it was available at etsy.com). It captures the kind of joy experienced by these two blessed women better than any rendering I've ever seen. This is a profound moment of *Yes!*

When Mary hears from the angel that Elizabeth is with child, she apparently drops everything in order to be of help. She has doubtless known and helped more than a few pregnant women in Nazareth up to this time, but now, understanding the greater need of a woman beyond the normal age to be with child, she is anxious to supply any assistance she can. Though she is to be the mother of the Messiah, to be the 'queen-mother' as it were, a position of great honor and dignity, she humbly thinks only of her kinswoman.

Mary and Elizabeth aren't strangers; I imagine that they have spent time together in the past, perhaps meeting after pilgrimages to Jerusalem for the great feasts, and that they are well known to each other. Elizabeth, a wise and faithful daughter of the covenant, might well be like a second mother to Mary. Their mutual love for the God of Abraham binds them even more closely than their blood kinship.

My speculation is that Mary's arrival isn't unexpected. Gabriel may well have informed Elizabeth, but when Mary greets Elizabeth it is a moment of deep grace for all. John, still in his mother's womb, is blessed to know that the one he will proclaim has come! He leaps for joy, and Elizabeth is aware this is not just a normal stirring of an unborn child but something more, and she is filled with the same joy: "Blessed are you among women and blessed is the fruit of your womb!"

Elizabeth knows and her unborn child knows what can only be known by the revelation of God. The Word has been made flesh and is present in the body of a sinless virgin. Mary is the mother of Elizabeth's lord, and they rejoice together in the blessings bestowed on them both, undreamed of graces from a God who has loved them both from eternity.

There would, I imagine, have been much laughter in the next three months as they spoke of their relatives and friends and shared the news of goings on in Galilee and Judea, and Mary would have helped by cooking and cleaning and anticipating Elizabeth's needs. It is unquestionable that she rejoiced with Elizabeth and Zechariah at the child's birth and stood up for and supported Elizabeth when she wanted to call him "John" though the neighbors and family resisted until Zechariah wrote "John is his name" and was given the gift of speech again and blessed God abundantly.

Finally, knowing that this was Zechariah and Elizabeth's day—and not her own—she slipped away with an embrace to both and probably a kiss to John and returned to Nazareth.

May we serve those who are in need in accord with our abilities and not so that we may be praised, but simply because it is God's will for us.

The Nativity

BACK IN NAZARETH COMES A MORE DIFFICULT *YES!* JOSEPH has probably known Mary all her life and knows her as a moral and obedient daughter to Joachim and Anna and a good friend and helper to many in their little town. He knows, too, that she is a faithful daughter, as he himself is a faithful son, to the Law as given by God to Moses. I have no doubt that he loves her and longs to take her as his wife in accord with the betrothal they celebrated some months ago. But he is chagrined when he finds her with child on her return from Judea. He knows she would not have been unfaithful to their betrothal vows, but still he knows the child cannot be his.

What thoughts must have entered his mind! How can this be? Pondering this question, he makes a decision. Knowing that if he denounces her she will be subject to stoning, he decides to give her a *get*, a divorce, to prevent her public shaming. But God has planned something better. An angel, probably Gabriel himself, comes to Joseph in a dream, a dream so real Joseph knows it is an authentic message from God. "Do not fear to take Mary as your wife," Gabriel tells him. "The child she carries has been conceived by the Holy Spirit. You are to be his father and you are to name him Jesus."

His fears are dispelled, and he says *Yes!* He takes Mary as his wife and will be this child's father in love if not by blood. He obeys God and he also obeys Caesar as he calls for the census and takes Mary to his ancestral home of Bethlehem. Not finding a place with some privacy he accepts the offer of a stable, dry and warm. There, perhaps without a midwife, Mary continues her *Yes!* and gives birth to a child she has already loved for nine months; she will love him even more as she embraces him and holds him to her breast. Joseph, likewise, loves this child and wordlessly takes him to his heart as his own. This tiny child is laid in a manger as his crib.

This is a most appropriate place, even though Joseph would rather he sleep in a crib he had made, for this Jesus, to whom Joseph will give that name, will become food, not for beasts, but for God's own people. Mary and Joseph also say *Yes!* at the wonder of shepherds who come to pay Jesus homage and at their story of angelic hosts who have announced his birth. No less than Mary, Joseph too will reflect upon these remarkable events all his days and give thanks that God chose him, and he will be a most faithful guardian to Mary and to her son, to his son, too.

May we be open to God's grace that we may bring Jesus' love and mercy into our world today.

The Presentation in the Temple

JOSEPH AND MARY ARE FILLED WITH PRIDE AS THEY TAKE their child to the temple. According to Mosaic Law, Jesus must be redeemed by a sacrifice because he is a firstborn son. They plan to offer the sacrifice of the poor, a pair of turtledoves or two young pigeons, and Joseph is humbled—a little—that he cannot offer the greater sacrifice of a sheep, but he is honest and hard-working and this is all their family can afford as he has had to work his trade in Bethlehem, far from their home in Nazareth.

As they approach, they are met by Simeon, an old man who asks to see almost every firstborn. Without fear Mary allows him to take Jesus in his arms and his face is transfigured in joy. God has revealed to him—we know not how—that he should not die until he has seen the Messiah. Simeon proclaims, "Now, Lord, you may let your servant go in peace for my eyes have seen the salvation you have prepared in the sight of your people!" He knows that this child *is* the Messiah and while the Messiah's glory is hidden now, he knows that all will be fulfilled in God's own time. His *Yes!* affirms for Mary and Joseph what they have already come to understand.

But he continues, filled with God's spirit of prophetic truth, and testifies to Jesus' mission for the fall and rise of many of God's people and that his ministry will be difficult and fraught with opposition. He also speaks chilling words to Mary which, I think, she has already begun to understand, that a sword should pierce her heart to allow the thoughts of many hearts to be revealed. She, too, says *Yes!* in the depths of her heart already given so completely to God and to His Son who is also her son.

She and Joseph will rejoice at these events with pride that they have been given this child and that they have given him to God's people. I imagine they will speak of these things often in the days to come, wondering at God's plan and giving thanks to Him that they have been given their own part in the plan and are playing it fully.

May we seek to know God's will for us, even though we know it may be difficult, allowing His grace to make up what is lacking in our own efforts.

The Finding in the Temple

A CHILD, EVEN ONE WHO IS BOTH GOD AND MAN, CAN act like a child. This is what happens here and what leads to another *Yes!* He has come with his parents to the feast and moved by grace, perhaps as he had never been before, is filled with zeal for the temple which is the place where his Father dwells in a most unique way.

Jesus knows he has a mission. He knows he is God's son in a way no other has ever been—how could he not? With a human mind that had to learn step-by-step as we have had to do, but he still possesses the divine nature with all the knowledge of his omniscient Father. How one person can be God and Man and how limited human and infinite divine knowledge can subsist in one intellect is an imponderable mystery.

The child Jesus is so filled with zeal that he wishes to begin his mission *right now*—and says *Yes!* right now—to that mission and to his Father's will even though it is not the right time. With the confusion of preparations to return to Galilee and Nazareth with the rest of the pilgrims, and with Jesus being of an age to travel either with the men or the women, it's easy for him to slip away. His absence goes unnoticed until Mary and Joseph come back together at the end of the first day's journey and realize that he's not there!

I don't think they start to worry immediately; after all he's probably with some of their relatives and friends. But after a diligent search, not finding him they begin to fear the worst. With the good wishes and the tearful prayers of their companions, they begin their return to Jerusalem. What all parents feel when they lose track of a child for more than a few moments, this is what Mary and Joseph felt. They *have* to find him!

Jerusalem is nothing like their little village where everyone knows everyone else; it's a bustling city of thousands with wide streets and narrow alleys and with all manner of people both good and evil. Night has fallen by the time they arrive, and the darkness is barely dispelled by their torchlight. What has happened to their son? They seek him where they had camped with their pilgrimage companions until night makes it impossible to continue. I doubt that either Joseph or Mary got more than a moment's sleep before dawn enables them to resume their quest. A whole day goes by fruitlessly, and both grow even more fearful until night falls again. Their prayers, already fervent as they have always been, grow even more desperate until they decide, at sundown, to begin the next day's search at the temple.

The Court of the Gentiles is crowded as usual with a wide variety of souls. There are pilgrims from the distant corners of the world, faithful Jews who marvel at the beauty surrounding them, buyers and sellers of all kinds of things for sacrifices, curious Gentiles who want to see where people who worship only one god offer sacrifices, Roman soldiers and temple guards patrolling to keep order, and people using this court as a shortcut into the city from the Mount of Olives. In the porticoes there are knots of people discussing matters both secular and religious, but in one portico a larger group of scribes and doctors of the law have gathered in a circle obviously paying rapt attention to someone in their midst.

Moved by grace, Joseph and Mary approach and hear the familiar voice of their son. He is speaking to these scholars with wisdom beyond his years and the scholars are amazed at his answers.

Mary approaches with Joseph and tearfully asks, "Where have you been? Don't you know we've been searching for you? Why have you done this?"

His response is honest but baffling: "Don't you know I have to be in my Father's house?"

They embrace him with strong arms and many tears and tell him it's time to return home as the scholars slowly disperse. Jesus understands that while his zeal today is good and real, he needs greater wisdom and he's not ready yet to take up his mission. He returns to Nazareth obediently to continue to learn from both of them the faithfulness that must mature in him with a resigned but heartfelt *Yes!* to them and, in doing so was saying *Yes!* as always to his Father's Will.

May we be filled with zeal for the proclamation of God's mercy and with joy that He can use us to make that mercy known.

The Luminous Mysteries

INTRODUCTION

IN 2002, POPE SAINT JOHN PAUL II WROTE AN APOSTOLIC letter titled *Rosarium Virginis Mariae* or *The Rosary of the Virgin Mary*. It was an addition to the many papal documents on the Rosary over centuries. Mary's rosary is probably the single most popular devotion of the Church's prayer besides the Mass and the Liturgy of the Hours (Divine Office) which are "official" prayers. Indeed, without the Mass, the Church would starve to death deprived of the Lord's Body and Blood as true food.

Many people welcomed the pope's document; it was a testimony to his own personal devotion to Mary which is manifest in his papal coat of arms with the prominent "M" and the motto: *Totus Tuus*—Totally Yours. His personal use of the rosary to pray is also clearly demonstrated. However, some people resisted part of the letter, his addition of another set of Mysteries to the Joyful, Sorrowful, and Glorious Mysteries. I find it difficult to understand these reservations.

No one, save perhaps consecrated religious by their particular rule, is ***obliged*** to pray the Rosary (even though Mary has asked us to do so at Fatima and many popes and bishops and priests and religious have often made the same request). Neither are there any particular regulations about how it is to be prayed. By venerable tradition one would pray the Joyful Mysteries on Monday and Thursday and on the Sundays of Advent and Christmas, the Sorrowful Mysteries on Tuesday and Friday and on the Sundays of Lent, and the Glorious Mysteries on Wednesday and Saturday and on the Sundays of Ordinary Time. But one is free to pray in the way he or she finds most helpful. I generally follow the tradition above but on particular feasts would pray the mysteries that included the feast. For example, I'd pray the Joyful Mysteries on the feasts of the Annunciation and Visitation and Glorious on the feasts of the Assumption and the Coronation.

The Luminous Mysteries or "Mysteries of Light," in my opinion, fill a gap between the Joyful and Sorrowful Mysteries. I personally find them to be a beautiful addition and a rich source of inspiration to me. Jesus lived a hidden life of almost twenty years between his return to Nazareth after being found in the temple and the beginning of his ministry, and this will remain hidden, I expect, until we meet him in Heaven. But there are events spoken of in the gospels that may help us understand him a bit more deeply and to understand some of the people close to him in those days. Can we not reflect on them in the context of the Rosary? Can they not help to deepen our rejoicing in the mercies God has shown us?

It's my hope that the "Yesses" revealed in these mysteries may help us to respond with greater and more fervent "Yesses" in our own lives.

If you pray the Rosary daily, God bless you! If you don't pray the Rosary daily, I hope you begin to do so, but even if the Rosary is only an occasional prayer, I suggest that you use the Luminous Mysteries on Thursday or at least consider doing so. I'm hopeful that you'll find them as helpful as I do.

The Luminous Mysteries
JESUS' BAPTISM

JESUS' CHILDLIKE ZEAL HAS NOT ABATED; IT HAS GROWN AND matured. Growing up in a loving and joyful family has helped him to become the man he is. He has learned much from Joseph. He has learned the carpenter's trade, but even more he has learned how to be a man, a son of the Covenant. He has learned respect for arduous work and respect for women and for those in need. He has learned how to take his place in the synagogue and to join in the prayers and practices proper to his state in life.

He has also learned how to grieve at the death of relatives and friends and especially at the death of Joseph himself. Tears flowed without shame when this man who called Jesus his son was called back to the God who made him. Jesus was now to be the rock and support to his mother as Joseph had been and to provide for her as Joseph had done even as he prepared to take up the ministry God had prepared for him.

The news of a prophet baptizing in the Jordan has certainly reached Nazareth; it's well known throughout Judea and Galilee and Jesus knows this prophet, John, his kinsman. Mary has told Jesus about John and the circumstances of his birth, and they have probably met at least a few times in childhood but not since John began his own ministry some years earlier, preaching repentance and preparation for the Messiah's coming. Jesus decides to start his own ministry with John's.

Jesus wants to identify with the people he's been sent to serve, and though he is sinless and without need to repent, he makes the days-long journey to John's place in the desert across the Jordan near Jericho. He listens and is moved by John's preaching—it reminds him of Elijah's fiery words—and approaches the water. Jesus' *Yes!* is a surrender to his Father's will to call his people and all people back to him, to life, to a relationship that will give life that will never end.

But John, who recognized Jesus and leapt for joy while both were in their mothers' wombs, understands fully that *this* is the one he was sent to herald. "You should be baptizing me," he says, in the fullest humility. "I'm not worthy to loosen your sandal straps!"

"John," Jesus replies, "this is the way it must be. It's my Father's will."

He still doesn't understand; it is beyond human understanding. His every instinct tells him it isn't right, but he trusts the one he has come to proclaim. With great care and profound love, realizing that he must decrease while Jesus increases, he says *Yes!* and pours the Jordan's water over the one who makes the water holy. The Spirit descends upon Jesus as a dove, and the Father proclaims Jesus as His Son, and as his ministry draws to its close, John can now proclaim, "Behold! There is the Lamb of God!"

May God grant us the grace to do His Will even when we do not understand His Will.

The Wedding Feast at Cana

THE "YESSES" HERE HAVE TO DO WITH A MOTHER'S LOVE for her son, as well as her love for others, and with a son's love for his mother. Mary has come with Jesus to a wedding feast. It is probably a relative who has married and, in accordance with the custom, who invites many to celebrate. The couple has probably been betrothed for at least a year or two, living with their families while they prepare a home where they will live after marriage. Preparations for the feast have been extensive, but, for whatever reason, the wine begins to run short.

Living in a small town where nothing much happens out of the ordinary, such a social blunder will probably be a source of gossip and not a little embarrassment for years. Mary loves these people who are not just friends but also kin and noticing—as a mother would—she goes to her son and simply tells him, "They have no more wine." She knows her son better than anyone else can or will and knows what he is capable of.

Jesus' response, however, seems cold and unfeeling and not a little disrespectful: "Woman, what has this to do with us? It is not yet my time."

Mary understands his love for her and his profound respect as any son should have for a beloved mother and knows his form of address is polite but formal. She doesn't confront him or chide him or try to cajole him; she knows his heart for it was formed in her womb and formed also by the love he learned from her and from Joseph and from the love Mary and Joseph had for each other. Her response is simply to tell the servants, "Do whatever he tells you," knowing that something remarkable will occur.

Her *Yes!* is first to an awareness of the couple's need, but it is also to a trusting in her son's compassion and mercy. She knows that the Will of God *will* be accomplished and allows Him to work in the way *He* chooses in and through His Son. The servants also say *Yes!* as they are called to do, making clear that obedience is the important thing, even if those who act in obedience don't understand the why or how.

Jesus loves his mother perfectly and has loved her even before— eternally before—her *fiat* allowed him to become incarnate. While this wedding feast isn't the time he would have chosen to manifest himself, now *is* the time. His *Yes!* is to his mother and to her care and it is a *Yes!* to charity and it turns water into choice wine, better than what had been served before.

The "Yesses" of mother and son, and even of the servants, challenge us to say yes in obedience at this moment, *now*, and not to wait for some perfect moment in the future to act with mercy.

May we be attentive to the need of the moment so that we may act in the present and not wait for a perfect time to act with mercy.

The Proclamation of the Gospel

JESUS' LIFE UP TO THIS POINT HAS BEEN RELATIVELY uneventful. True he was taken in the dead of night as an exile to Egypt and dwelt there in the Jewish community with Mary and Joseph until their return to Nazareth, and he gave his parents a scare when he stayed behind in Jerusalem when he was twelve, but we don't know much else about him. I expect that he lived much like the boys of his age, playing games in the streets, learning to read in the synagogue school, learning Joseph's trade, but besides his obedience and charity he wouldn't have distinguished himself much.

The Apocryphal Gospels that tell of his working miracles like making birds out of clay and clapping his hands to make them fly away are an attempt to fill in the hidden years but, I think, they ring hollow. Had Jesus been a miracle worker from his childhood, his ministry might well have been more readily accepted by his neighbors.

Now, however, is the time. He has a passionate love for his Father and the Holy Spirit, and he shares Their passionate love for the people of the Covenant. It is the desire of his heart to tell them of the Father's love so that their response to that love might go beyond the demands of the Law. So he begins to preach as the *Yes!* of this mystery.

Even were he not God, he would understand that many would resist his message, and he is saddened by their hard hearts. His own heart must break when he sees the word snatched away from the hearts and minds of his hearers.

Some have come because he is a curiosity, unschooled, not of any of the religious sects like Pharisees, Sadducees, and Essenes. He doesn't preach using fancy words or lofty rhetoric but uses parables that speak of the realities of his audience's lives, shepherds, farmers, wives and mothers. He appeals to their hearts and challenges them to put their hearts' decisions into actions. Neither does he speak like the rabbis who quote various predecessors on several sides of a question but with his own authority: "But *I* say to you . . ."

He works miracles for the crowds to manifest the mercy he proclaims, the desire of His Father to dwell with and in them. He has to respond to the challenges of the scribes who oppose him, almost at every turn.

Knowing that he cannot work alone, he gathers disciples, some of whom he knows will abandon him and he prays that their faith may not fail. Discouragement tempts him to give up, but he will not. He wanders from place to place, often sleeping in the fields, but always follows the direction of the Spirit. His *Yes!* is renewed over and over again each day, and sometimes each hour, that his Word will touch hearts and lead those hearts to His Father.

May we proclaim the Good News boldly, by our actions and even by our words even if others do not wish to listen.

The Transfiguration

MOUNT TABOR ISN'T TERRIBLY HIGH, ONLY ABOUT 1,900 feet in elevation, but it stands out starkly from the surrounding plain. It's not surprising that Jesus would choose it as a place to reveal his glory, much like God used Sinai to reveal Himself to Moses. I imagine it was something of a climb for Jesus and Peter, James, and John, but he chose them, his 'inner circle,' so that he might prepare them by a special revelation for the coming scandal of the crucifixion.

He has made the climb for prayer—this is always Jesus' *Yes!* —it is an intimate conversation with his Father and the Holy Spirit, and to teach these apostles something about prayer so that they could teach their brothers in turn. But they are wearied by their journey and fall asleep. Upon awaking they see Jesus. It is unquestionably him, but he's been changed. His clothing is whiter than anything they've ever seen and Jesus himself is brighter than the noonday sun, and yet they can look upon him without shielding their eyes. With him are two men, likewise glorified, but obviously not his equals. One holds the stone tablets of The Law and the other stands upon a chariot of fire. The apostles understand that these two are Moses and Elijah; Jesus is talking with them about the fulfillment of The Law and The Prophets, his own Exodus to come in Jerusalem.

Baffled and bewildered, Peter, James, and John look on in amazement, and Peter, with his accustomed zeal, speaks without thinking first. "Master, it is good for us to be here! Let us build three tabernacles to commemorate this, one for you and one for Moses and one for Elijah."

At that, a cloud came, casting a shadow on them, frightening them, and from the cloud comes a voice, the very voice of the Father: "This is my beloved Son. **Listen** to *Him*!" He tells them that this is not the time to speak but this is the time for them to listen.

The three cower in the shadow until Jesus approaches, looking as he had before their climb, touches them and bids them to return to the others at the bottom of the mount. He tells them not to speak of this to the rest until he has been raised and they are obedient, but they still will not understand for some time.

Jesus' *Yes!* to the Transfiguration is for the three to be strengthened, a little, when they find he's been arrested and condemned and crucified, but I think it's also for Jesus himself. He knows, far better than anyone could imagine, what is coming for him. As a man, a reasonable man, he is at least apprehensive if not inwardly terrified about what is to come and so his Father reminds him who he is, the beloved only-begotten Son who has been with Him and the Spirit from eternity who was the One testified to by The Law and The Prophets and that after his death he would be raised up and glorified.

May we be transformed by grace every day to manifest God's presence by our charity.

The Institution of the Eucharist

THIS MYSTERY IS, IN SOME WAYS, THE GREATEST YES! OF them all. Speaking of time makes no sense when discussing eternity. God is, as the Triune Creator of all that is, also the creator of time, and all moments are one for Him who is outside of time. Yet by the infinite mercy of God's Will He makes it possible for those limited by time to participate in His own eternity. This we do in a remarkable way in the Eucharist. In a specific moment of time we are invited to receive into our own bodies and spirits, the glorified Body and Blood of Christ, who is eternal God and to be one with him *in* eternity. We can never be closer to Him in this world than when He enters our bodies.

Jesus gathers in the upper room with his twelve closest friends. He has taught them at length of the Father's love and has shown that love in myriad ways. Even were he not God, he was perceptive enough as a man to see what was coming. This was the Passover feast, and the city was filled to overflowing with pilgrims from the whole of the Roman world. He knew this was the time ordained to replace the yearly sacrifice of a lamb with a new sacrifice, once for all, of Himself as the paschal Lamb of God. He also knew of the weak faith of these twelve and that one, in fact, still dearly loved, would betray him for 30 pieces of silver. His heart is filled with love for all of them, but there is also a great sadness in this gathering; he knows it is their last.

Nevertheless, he celebrates a new Seder meal and taking bread and breaking it gives it to the twelve and says, "Take and eat this. This *is* my Body." These are strange words, not part of the official 'script' for this ritual meal. They take and eat what was once bread, puzzled by the words. Did they understand what had just happened? Did they know it was no longer bread?

At the end of the meal Jesus again departs from the ritual. Taking wine, he says, "Take and drink from this, all of you, because this is the new Covenant in my Blood, poured out for you. Do this in memory of me." Again they drink, still puzzled perhaps, but understanding this is something new and more meaningful than they could know at this time.

Jesus says *Yes!* to his Father in his self-gift and *Yes!* to his apostles, too. He wants them to know him even more intimately and to know the Father and Holy Spirit too; he becomes part of their very being in the simple elements of bread and wine. He wants them—and us—to live a new kind of life that only he can give and makes this new rite something that bears witness to what will happen on Good Friday and Easter Sunday and that will make it truly present until time itself will cease. Every Mass proclaims and brings about the Paschal Mystery and we are invited to join our "Amen," our *Yes!* to his.

May the Most Blessed Sacrament of Jesus' Body and Blood be the desire of our hearts each day that receiving Him we may make Him known.

The Sorrowful Mysteries
THE AGONY IN THE GARDEN

SOMETIMES A *YES!* IS GIVEN BOLDLY AND WITHOUT hesitation, as Mary's yes to visit and assist Elizabeth. The "Yesses" that come in the Sorrowful Mysteries, however, are much more difficult. Jesus' humanity, while always in harmony with his divine nature, naturally resists what will cause him to suffer as no one else in our history could suffer or can suffer. His sufferings encompass all the sufferings of humankind from its beginning until time itself shall cease.

Jesus has celebrated the Seder for the last time with his apostles and has given them his Flesh and Blood as food and drink although they probably had little or no understanding of this profound grace of that moment. He has sent Judas to complete his betrayal after showing Judas that he's still loved by Jesus giving him the morsel he himself has dipped. He and the eleven sing the Hallel psalms of praise to the Father although he, doubtless, sings with sadness, as they approach Gethsemane.

Knowing what is before him, he asks the group to pray and invites Peter, James, and John to come with him as he goes deeper into the garden, again inviting them to keep prayerful watch and stay awake as he prays. One traditional picture shows him kneeling at a rock, almost as a *prie-dieu*, but I think he stood and walked about in his prayer; his anxiety was too great for him to stand still until at last he falls to the ground.

He humbly asks his Father to allow this cup to pass him by. He understands, even just from his humanity, what's about to come. He is to be arrested by his enemies and can expect no kindness from them, even though he passionately loves them. They will hand him over to the governor for crucifixion. Jesus knows about crucifixion; he has probably seen criminals and rebels crucified along the roadsides even as a child and was always filled with compassion for them, praying for them and wanting to ease their sufferings if he could. Knowing what is about to happen, he again asks his Father to let this cup pass by but says, "Not my will but Yours be done." Jesus doesn't want this, but he *wills* this; *this* is his *Yes!* given reluctantly, I believe, but still given wholeheartedly again and again.

Returning to the three apostles, he finds them sleeping and while troubled by this still loves them and wakes them, again asking them to keep watch. He prays as he did before, again returning to find them sleeping. The third time he wakes them and tells them it is time. Judas and the temple guards have come to put him in custody. He will be betrayed by one he loves, but he still says *Yes!*

May we know God's presence in our times of desolation and anxiety that we may be strengthened to bear our sufferings in peace and in joy.

The Scourging at the Pillar

AFTER HIS EXAMINATION AND CONDEMNATION BY THE Sanhedrin in an illegal trial (for it took place at night), during which he was roundly mocked, abused, and beaten, he is taken by the Sanhedrin to Pilate, the Roman Procurator. Pilate is not necessarily an evil man, but he has learned to govern in Rome's name with Roman harshness and brutality. All he understands of the Sanhedrin's charges is that they are jealous of this teacher whom they believe is an unschooled upstart and heretic. He has heard about this Jesus for several years and has discounted the claims of his being seditious. Knowing that this prisoner, whom he can tell has already been subject to physical abuse, hasn't committed a crime under Roman law, Pilate wants to acquit him. The persistent pleas of these Jews, however, frighten him with the prospect of revolt, especially as the city is filled with Jewish pilgrims. He then sentences him to be flogged.

Jesus may never have witnessed a scourging but has doubtless seen its results in the scars born by slaves and other prisoners. He is afraid, and for good reason. Scourging is a punishment sometimes employed by his own people, but Roman scourging is far worse. The end of each flail of the flagellum has imbedded in it metal or bone that grabs the flesh and pulls it away at the end of each stroke. He knows that people have died from scourging and subsequent loss of blood. Pilate has not specified the number of lashes, leaving it to the merciless judgment of the prison detail.

Fearful, but still filled with a spirit of obedience to his Father, although his Father seems very far away, he submits. He says *Yes!* for love of Him and because of his love for his people and even for these pagans whom he wants to gather into his Father's house.

Stripped of everything but a loincloth, he is chained to a pillar and the soldiers begin. The first stroke takes his breath away in a gasp of pain that he's never experienced before; as the whip is withdrawn pieces of his flesh are ripped away and he begins to bleed. A second stroke from the other side simply intensifies the agony. At each blow he grunts and pants, finding it hard to breathe, and yet he still says *Yes!* for all who have suffered and will suffer. He loses count of the number of lashes, but he wordlessly forgives his tormentors.

Can the blood and flesh that spatter the detachment of soldiers who watch in boredom—they have seen this many times before—touch some of their hearts in the days to come? Will they come to believe in his forgiveness as it will be preached by his apostles? Only he himself and his Father and Holy Spirit can know.

May we allow our sufferings, physical, mental, and emotional, to be filled with grace to sustain us in Christ's love.

The Crowning with Thorns

NONE OF US LIKE BEING RIDICULED AND MOCKED. EVEN when we're being mildly joshed by family and friends we can become uncomfortable, but this is as different from that as any contradictions we can imagine.

Very few (if any) of the Roman soldiers attached to the garrison in Jerusalem wanted to be there. Palestine was at best a backwater. It was far from the centers of culture and even farther from the centers of imperial power. The amusements available to soldiers were limited, especially since the Jews were particularly obstinate in their hatred of Rome. Most conquered peoples submitted fairly well, and their native religions fit well in the Roman Pantheon. But these Jews wouldn't even burn incense to the Emperor and claimed that there was only one God and that Rome's gods weren't gods at all!

Mocking a Jewish prisoner was something of a diversion for them, especially since he had claimed to be king of the Jews. One of their number created a kind of cap out of the long thorns of a scrub plant (sticking himself several times even through his leather gloves) to place on the scourged prisoner's head as a crown. Another took one of their military robes and put it around his shoulders and put a reed in his hand as a scepter; all began to ridicule him as "King of the Jews" spitting at him and striking him as they did so.

Blood flowed freely from the thorns practically blinding him as he bore this ridicule. He knew what would come next at the hands of these very soldiers, and yet still he loved them, in spite of all their abuse. Jesus knew that he was a king but was no threat to any human king or emperor. Some of these men might even come to acknowledge his kingship without mockery, but for now, all he could do in the midst of physical and emotional anguish was to give himself to his Father's Will and say *Yes!* to the suffering that he had to endure in this moment and to pray for these and for those who had handed him over. And this *Yes!* would become even more difficult.

May our difficulties be crowned by grace and borne with joy as we unite our sufferings to the suffering of Christ's Body on earth.

The Way of the Cross

PILATE CALLS FOR JESUS AND HE IS BROUGHT FROM THE holding area. Even Pilate is amazed at the man who stands before him, still wearing the crown of thorns and staggering from the torment of the scourging. The governor presents him to the crowd: "Behold the man!" Many, even his rabid enemies, are astonished and gasp at the sight but jeer him, and still the Elders call for his execution. Some few, like his mother and Magdalene and John, weep to see him so badly treated. Even some who don't believe in him think this is too much.

Pilate wishes to release him, but the Sanhedrin prompt the crowd to call out "Crucify him!" again and again until the governor relents in fear of a riot he cannot control.

Signaling for silence he calls for water and washes his hands of judgment and says, "Crucify him yourselves! His blood is on your hands."

The leaders of Jesus' people reply, "His blood be on us and on our children." His blood *is* their blood; he is of their stock, like them a child of Abraham, Isaac, and Jacob. And although they don't know it, that blood is poured out to save them. The soldiers take Jesus and the two thieves to the hill of Golgotha, Skull Place, each carrying his own crossbeam.

Weakened by thirst and loss of blood, discouraged by the rejection of so many of his own beloved people, he begins a slow march to his place of execution. He does not feel his Father's presence and hasn't for some time, and yet he knows He is there. Jesus knows the love he cannot feel is still present and he knows this is part of what was planned even before the sin of Adam. He must walk this path and says *Yes!* with every step. The road is crowded with spectators on all sides, some jeering and spitting and some weeping.

As he stumbles and falls, the detachment of soldiers fear he will die before he can be crucified and press Simon into service to carry the cross. Simon is given no choice by the soldiers, but when he looks into Jesus' eyes he is moved by the pain but also by love he sees there for him—it is as if he has been known by this man all his life—and with his own *Yes!* gladly takes up the burden. When he comes to the place of execution, instead of leaving the cross and fleeing, he stays and finds himself in the group of those who love Jesus; Mary thanks him for helping her son and Simon is changed forever.

May we undertake our daily tasks, even the most difficult and unpleasant, with joy in Christ's presence.

The Crucifixion

THE *YES!* HERE IS ABSOLUTELY ESSENTIAL FOR OUR SALVATION and justification. Was it possible to have been accomplished in some other way? I have found it unwise to declare that God cannot do something, but this was, in fact, the way that the Trinity decided that salvation should be accomplished, that Adam's sin should be undone by a Son of Adam, a *new* Adam.

Crucifixion is truly an ignominious form of execution—as if any form of execution could be pleasant or painless. In some *"modern"* and *"enlightened"* societies we have developed quicker ways, maybe with less physical pain (but always with great emotional suffering), but capital punishment remains, in my opinion, contemptible and inhumane.

Once a man or woman was fixed to the cross, death could take hours or even days, and the suffering is literally excruciating. The relatively quick death that Jesus experienced (about three hours) was the exception rather than the rule. He had sweated blood at Gethsemane, been beaten at the house of the high priest, flogged mercilessly by the Romans, crowned with thorns, and was suffering a great loss of blood from these tortures—and probably had been given nothing to drink for hours—then was forced to walk to his place of execution. Being nailed to the cross was simply the end of the beginning of his death.

Jesus' sufferings were truly indescribable. He suffered intense physical pain, of course, but suffered emotionally as well. He felt abandoned by his closest friends, but even worse felt he had been abandoned by his Father. How else could he cry out from the cross, "My God, my God, why have you forsaken me?" Certainly as God he knew that he was with his Father and his Father with him, but he was also truly human and subject to the same doubts all of us possess. Did he *know* God was with him? Of course. Did he still *feel* alone? Yes. But he continued to say *Yes!* for our salvation and for love of his Father

From the cross he forgives his executioners, something that shakes them to the core. They expected—and had usually received—curses and threats from their victims, but forgiveness is the last thing they could have imagined. There is a legend that the soldier who won Jesus' seamless robe eventually came to believe in the one who had worn it, but I also wonder—and hope—that at least a few soldiers would finally come to understand his forgiveness and to seek it as his followers.

Jesus also forgives those who, out of needless fear, sought to end his teaching by ending his life. Might some of them have repented? He forgives his frightened apostles, even Peter who had denied him three times, and prays even for Judas who had betrayed him.

He says "I thirst" to fulfill the scriptures but mostly because he thirsts for our love. When mocked and reviled by one thief, he is asked by the other to be remembered when he comes into his kingdom; Jesus promises that the thief will be with him in paradise this very day.

When the soldiers finally allow the spectators near, Mary comes to the foot of the cross with John and Magdalene and maybe some of the other women who have shown more courage than Peter and the rest. Jesus' love for his mother is as it has ever been, pure and undiminished, but he will not be able to care for her any longer in this world. "Woman," he says, "*there* is your son," indicating John, and to him, "There is your mother." Mary now knows fully what Simeon had said on the joyful day of his presentation in the temple, for a sword now truly pierces her immaculate heart and yet for love of her son says *Yes!* and John says *Yes!* as well.

As the time drags on, he understands that what has been the divine plan before creation began has come to its completion and says, "It is finished." And finally, in a loud voice testifies, "Father, into your hands I commend my spirit," not just dying but with his last mortal breath saying *Yes!* to his Father for our salvation and delivers over his spirit.

May we embrace the daily dying to self that leads to our sharing in the Resurrection of Jesus.

The Glorious Mysteries
THE RESURRECTION

The strife is o'er, the battle done.

WHEN JESUS DIED ON THE CROSS, HIS MORTAL BODY WAS buried in a borrowed tomb. But his soul is set free. He can see his Father and the Holy Spirit face-to-face once again and what a reunion that must have been! But the 'harrowing of Hell' must still take place, and he says *Yes!* to this great task as he breaks the gates of the Limbo of the Fathers' to bring those souls who had waited so long to the reward of Heaven. I think the first to greet him was Joseph, whom Jesus had loved as a father on Earth and who rejoiced to see the one he was proud to call his son. I imagine his first question was "How is your mother?"

He greets John, his kinsman, by whom he had been baptized. He greets John's parents, Zechariah and Elizabeth, as well as his own grandparents. He welcomes and is welcomed by the whole host of prophets and patriarchs from Abraham and Isaac to Moses and Elijah, who had appeared with him on Tabor. He also takes by their wrists Adam and Eve—whose hands were too weak, whose joyful tears flow ceaselessly as he leads them to the gates of Heaven which their sin had shut fast. The choirs of angels sing with profound joy while Lucifer and his angels cower in the presence of Light from Light.

But Jesus' *Yes!* is not finished. I think he would have been humanly satisfied to remain in Heaven forever, but he still obeys, as he always has. A new kind of life comes to the body that had been tortured and defiled, and his body is transformed and glorified, never to experience pain again. This body, **his own body**, will no longer be limited by space and time. Locked doors will not bar him and neither will a stone and soldiers and an imperial Roman seal. He bursts from the tomb with light that outshines the midday sun and scatters the terrified guards. **He is risen; he is truly risen!**

The gospels omit many details that we might wish to know, but the Holy Spirit who inspired the evangelists chose to reveal that which is necessary for our salvation, not what is not. Nevertheless, it's my belief that Jesus did not appear first to Magdalene, but to Mary, his own mother. Mary was up early, as was her custom, and perhaps she was in prayer when Jesus, raised and glorified, stood before her. Unlike those who didn't recognize the risen Lord at first, Mary knew immediately this was her beloved son. How they must have laughed and rejoiced! Their tears were pure joy. She could do nothing less than her son, that is, to say *Yes!* to him and to the Father's Will, to rejoice in his conquest of death for her and for all who would call him "Lord" and for all who would call her "Mother."

Jesus then appeared in turn to Magdalene and some women and the disciples on the road to Emmaus. Perhaps his most significant appearance was to his apostles in the upper room on the very night of the resurrection. Greeting the ten (for Thomas was absent) with "Peace be with you!" he made it clear that he had not come to condemn them for their fear and cowardice but to commission them to forgive sin by his own authority. He ate with them to show he was no ghost, that his promise to rise again was no wishful thinking but absolute truth.

For the next forty days Jesus would continue to appear: in the upper room to call Thomas back to faith and at the Sea of Galilee to provide a miraculous catch of fish and to ask Peter to undo his denial by a three-fold profession of his love. He would continue to appear, although some of these instances have not been recorded, and to help them know that he was undeniably raised and that he would never die again. By his rising he called those who followed him to join in his own *Yes!* by proclaiming the truth that he who died had been raised and would come again in glory.

May we glory in Jesus' conquest of death that we may share that victory ourselves.

The Ascension

IN THIS GLORIOUS YES! I THINK THERE MAY BE A TINGE OF sadness for the risen Lord. He loves these apostles and disciples and the holy women who had followed him almost from the beginning. There is profound joy in him, even humanly, to be with them and to share their lives once more in the physical world that is their home. I believe he shared laughs with them many times before his passion. I envision, for example, Jesus and the twelve walking along the Jordan on a muggy day and glancing at them and at the river and finally saying something like "Last one in is a Pharisee!" as he runs to cool himself in the water and they follow. They splash and laugh and dunk one another in the water as if they haven't a reason in the world to do otherwise.

That laughter, I believe, continues as he appears to them now and again and continues to teach them his Father's love and his own love for them. But now he comes to a time of parting. He would love to stay with them as he has since his rising, but he understands that cannot be.

When he leaves them, of course, he will not abandon them in any way, but the manner of his presence will be different. Sometimes, however, they may still *feel* abandoned. They will long to see him as he is now and they will grieve that they cannot. From now on they will have to see him in each other and in those to whom they will share the good news. He knows that they still don't really understand; the Holy Spirit must fill them first. And so, he is saddened to say goodbye.

He has called the eleven to the mountain, where he had met with them many times before and some may perceive there is something different about this meeting. Looking upon them with love, he instructs them that they are not to leave Jerusalem but to wait there for the Holy Spirit. And he tells them to preach the Good News to all the nations and to baptize them in the name of the Father, in His name, and in the name of the Holy Spirit. Finally he tells them that although they shall not see him this way again, he will be with them, that he *is* with them until the end of the age. Then he says **Yes!** to his Father's will and is lifted up, disappearing into the clouds, ascending to sit at the Father's right hand forever.

Some of them are probably puzzled and expect him to return at any moment, but some understand they will not see him in this way again, but these, too, still look up. Finally, two angels instruct them: "Men of Galilee, why do you still look up to the sky? This Jesus whom you have seen taken up will return in the same way."

The eleven, some in tears, say **Yes!** and return to the upper room to pray to be clothed in power as Jesus has promised them, still pondering what all this has meant and fearful because they still do not understand.

May we remember that, although we cannot see Him, He is always present to the Church and to all of its members.

The Descent of the Holy Spirit

THIS *YES!* COMES FROM HEAVEN. IT IS IMPORTANT TO mention, I believe, that the three persons of the Trinity are always in perfect harmony, and while actions may be attributed to one person they are not performed independently. This is why Baptism in the name of the Creator, the Redeemer, and the Sanctifier is not valid. The Father *is* the Creator, but He creates in and through the Son in union with the Holy Spirit. God is Triune and each person is distinct, but no person acts without the other two persons. So it is in the event of Pentecost.

Jesus has told his disciples that if he does not return to his Father, he cannot send the Holy Spirit. The *Yes!* of the Ascension testifies to this. The Paraclete, the Advocate Jesus spoke of, will continue the Son's work until the end of time.

While the disciples and apostles were heartened to know of Jesus' resurrection, not as a "cleverly concocted myth" but as indisputable fact, yet they are still unsure about what to do now that Jesus is no longer physically present in his glorified body, even though they have heard the commission given them by the Lord before he ascended. They and others of Jesus' followers, Jesus' **believers**, spend time in the crowded upper room in prayer and reflection. I imagine they discuss how they are to preach to the nations and that there are more than a few disagreements.

Mary is there with them, with her quiet but steadying presence, praying confidently to her son whom she knows is far more than just her son. She seeks to encourage the rest, possibly sharing the insights she has gained from the time Gabriel first came to her and she responded with her *Yes!*

It is morning, the 50th day since Jesus rose, and they hear the sound of a strong driving wind that frightens them at first. Then fire, in the form of tongues, rests upon the head of each and burns out their fear. The heart of each one, apostle or disciple, male or female, is filled with understanding that makes so much that had fuddled them just moments before now abundantly clear.

They throw open the doors and windows—they will never have to be shut for fear again—and go out into the street. A crowd has gathered, drawn by the sound, and Peter and his brothers begin to proclaim what is true! Those who had been set aflame by the tongues bubble with such enthusiasm that the crowd believes they are drunk until, while speaking, their words touch hearts in the many different native languages the multitude spoke.

Peter speaks and his words are echoed by the apostles and disciples in many modes of speech and yet there is no confusion of languages; Babel has been undone! The assembly, moved by the enthusiasm of those who had formerly been fearful, come to hear truth and to understand the Truth—Jesus himself crucified and now risen—being proclaimed, and come to faith.

The Church is truly born this day, and Peter and the Eleven with him will never cease to announce Good News until silenced by their deaths. There will be obstacles they must face—persecution, imprisonment, and death—but they will continue to profess and proclaim the Gospel. Moved by the *Yes!* of Jesus sending the Spirit, moved by the *Yes!* of the Spirit Himself in descending as tongues of flame,

Mary—as she has already done many times—and Peter and James and John and the whole company of disciples, including those whose names we shall not know until we greet them in Heaven, say *Yes!* with enthusiasm zeal and joy as we are called to do today as well.

May the fire of the Holy Spirit destroy our fearfulness and strengthen us to bear bold witness to the Truth that is Christ Jesus.

The Assumption

THERE ARE A NUMBER OF THEOLOGIANS WHO MAINTAIN that Mary, not having been touched by original sin, therefore did not suffer physical death, which is one of the consequences of that sin. Many others believe (and I believe) that Mary did die. In fact, there are at least three places believed to have been her tomb, one is at the Latin Catholic Dormition Abbey in Jerusalem, another in the possession of the Greek Orthodox on the Mount of Olives, and a third in Ephesus. One of the apocryphal gospels writing of Mary's death says that all the twelve, with the exception of Thomas, were present when she died and buried her with great sadness and many tears. Just as Thomas was not present in the upper room on the evening of the resurrection and was present the following Sunday, he was a week late in coming to Mary and when he was brought by the other apostles to her grave, all found, to their wonder and astonishment, that the grave was empty; she had been assumed into Heaven.

Pope Pius XII solemnly defined Mary's Assumption in 1950 and stated that "when the course of her life on earth was completed, she was assumed into Heaven Body and Soul." This is the fourth Glorious

Mystery. While it was not dogmatically *defined* until the 20th century, it was something long believed by the Church and proclaimed by many esteemed teachers. It is another gracious *Yes!* by her son and one of his greatest gifts to her.

Mary's flesh, pure and untainted by any touch of sin or its effects, was the source of Jesus' sinless flesh. It was therefore unimaginable that her body would share the corruption of the tomb. Saint John Damascene, quoted by Pius XII, says:

"It was necessary that she who had preserved her virginity inviolate in childbirth should also have her body kept free from all corruption after death. It was necessary that she who carried the Creator on her breast should dwell in the tabernacles of God."

Even more, however, Jesus' love for her would not permit it. As he was present body and soul at the right hand of the Father in Heaven, she was to be present also.

God has created us to be creatures of body and soul, "amphibians" as Screwtape calls us in C. S. Lewis' *The Screwtape Letters*. I think that many believe that the body and soul are somehow separable parts. We are neither bodies *with* souls nor souls *with* bodies but *enfleshed* souls and *ensouled* bodies. It is the divine plan for us to be in Heaven whole and complete. Until the day of resurrection at the end of time, however, those who have passed from this life *are* disembodied. That is why we speak of the "souls in Heaven." By the most exceptional *Yes!* of her Son and of the Father and Holy Spirit, she is whole and complete, the model and example for us here on Earth; she is glorified as her son is glorified and as we shall be glorified if we die in a saving relationship with Jesus.

Mary would not have sought this grace. Her humility would not presume on the Father's Mercy to ask for such a gift, but having been given it she gives thanks and continues in her own *Yes!* to proclaim God's praise as she did when she visited Elizabeth. It can be our grace to echo her prayer each day: "My soul magnifies the Lord;

my spirit finds joy in God my Savior" both here on Earth and forever in Heaven.

May the example of Mary's yesses help us to cooperate with God's grace that we may come to share her glory in humility and gratitude.

The Coronation

MARY IS ASKED ONE MORE TIME IN THIS MYSTERY FOR *YES!*
God has another plan, or rather makes known a part of the plan made
from all eternity, for this most blessed among women. As Jesus from
the cross gave the beloved disciple to her as her son, he gives all of
his brothers and sisters to her as her children. He wishes her to take
a special role in the work of sanctification by the Holy Spirit.

Jesus asks her to be the queen of Heaven and Earth, but this can be
much misunderstood. Mary is, indeed, most blessed, but she is always—
and understands herself to be—a creature, not the Creator. She is not
God and would shrink from any who would give her the honor and worship that belongs only to the Father, Son, and Holy Spirit. As she says in
the Magnificat, "my spirit finds joy in God, my Savior." She knows whose
grace has kept her safe from Original Sin and from personal sin, God's
grace, which has come to her as a pure and unmerited gift.

Her son asks her to be a sign for the Church that is his body of
obedience and constant *Yes!* He wants her to be a sign of the glory
that he wants to share with all of us. He grants her the grace to hear
the prayers of her children, his brothers and sisters, and to intercede
with him—the one Mediator—for them.

For those who may feel too distant from Jesus because of fear or an awareness of their sinfulness (because he is the eternal God with the Father and Holy Spirit) she can show maternal care. She can seek her son's blessings for those who feel they dare not ask those blessings for themselves. As the queen, she sits near the throne of God ever praising Him with the angels and saints and ever beseeching His mercy on His children.

When Mary is asked to take on this ministry, she doesn't hesitate. She has always known the One who asks and that she owes everything to Him and to His grace. There is no question about her response: *Yes!* And that is her response given again and again as we ask her to "pray for us, sinners, now and at the hour of our death."

Father, Son and Holy Spirit, grant us the grace, through Mary, our Mother and Queen, to say *Yes!* each day until we can say *Yes!* in Heaven in the day that will never end.

May Mary's reigning with her Son as Queen of Heaven fill us with joy as a promise of our own share in the royal dignity of God's children.

Postscript

IT IS MY HOPE THAT YOU HAVE FOUND THESE REFLECTIONS helpful to an understanding (at least *my* understanding) of Mary's Rosary. Since the mysteries *are* mysteries, of course, there is no one absolutely perfectly right "explanation" of what is contained in them.

In the meantime, however, I encourage you, the reader, to consider the Mysteries of the Rosary not as academic subjects to debate and ponder, but as examples of the love of the Triune God to be reflected on in prayer. God loves us passionately and uniquely; there has never been and never will be another person exactly like you. Seek to understand that love as well as you can in prayer, asking the help first of all of the Holy Spirit, and then of Mary and Joseph, of Zechariah and Elizabeth and John the Baptist, of the apostles and of your patron saints to grow in that understanding.

Rejoice in that love and share it by the Corporal and Spiritual Works of Mercy and, of course, in the Church's greatest prayer, the Sacrifice of the Mass. Ask God to forgive your sins and to grant you a forgiving heart to forgive those who've sinned against you. Give praise to Father, Son, and Holy Spirit by every breath, proclaiming, as Mary did, *"My soul magnifies the Lord; my spirit finds joy in God my Savior."*